ECK WISDOM

on

Prayer,
Meditation,
and
Contemplation

ECK Wisdom
on
Prayer, Meditation, and Contemplation

HAROLD KLEMP

ECKANKAR
Minneapolis
Eckankar.org

ECK Wisdom on Prayer, Meditation, and Contemplation

Copyright © 2008 ECKANKAR

Printed in USA

Third printing—2022

Photo of Sri Harold Klemp (page 79) by Art Galbraith
Cover art by Claude Gruffy

Library of Congress Cataloging-in-Publication Data

Names: Klemp, Harold, author.
Title: ECK wisdom on prayer, meditation, and contemplation / Harold Klemp.
Description: Minneapolis: Eckankar, 2022.
Identifiers: LCCN 2022035864 | ISBN 9781570435331 (paperback)
Subjects: LCSH: Spiritual life--Eckankar.
Classification: LCC BP605.E3 K553856 2022 | DDC 299/.93--dc23/eng/20220908
LC record available at https://lccn.loc.gov/2022035864

♾ This paper meets the requirements of ANSI/NISO Z39.48-1992 (Permanence of Paper).

CONTENTS

RESPONDING TO THE CALL OF SOUL

*I*f you are a sincere seeker of truth, you realize that something within you is constantly pushing you from the nest. You know the answers you seek do exist somewhere in the world. This inner force that pushes you to find the answers is an urge you have no control over.

It is the call of Soul.

Prayer. Meditation. Contemplation. What's at the heart of these spiritual practices? Each is a response to the call of Soul. Each represents an individual's desire to contact the source of all truth. Different paths to reach the same goal.

You are Soul, a divine spark of God on a journey homeward. Soul wants to experience more of the Voice of God, which can be heard as Sound or seen as Light. So you begin your search.

In this book you will find keys to accelerate your pursuit of truth. You will read about the Spiritual Exercises of ECK, which are creative techniques taught by Eckankar, the Path of Spiritual Freedom. Insights from this study will enrich your spiritual journey, whatever your chosen path—your own response to the call of Soul.

DISCOVER THE
SOURCE OF ALL TRUTH

*L*earn to go inside yourself, because this is the source of all truth. There are a lot of holy temples out here, but the most sacred of all is the temple inside you, because this is where you meet with the Holy Spirit, the Voice of God.

How do you meet with the Holy Spirit?

If you're in Christianity, you pray. You come to the holy temple, to the holy of holies, through prayer. You meet on holy ground with your God. If you're a member of any other religion, you have a means of going to that holy of holies, whether it's meditation or contemplation or prayer.

Go to the holy of holies. It's the temple inside you. This is the place where all truth comes from. Before there were words, before there was a written Bible or a printed Gutenberg Bible, before there was Luther's translation, there was the Word in the heart of mankind.

This is the temple. Go there.

THE PURSUIT OF GOD

A search for happiness is the pursuit of God. Yet the reason so many people fail to find happiness is because they look for it in the wrong place—at the market instead of in their hearts.

It takes discipline to pursue God.

There is no mystery to finding God. Just follow the Sound of the divine Voice back home. Could anything be easier? Not so for most people, for whom the pursuit of God is as unlikely as the phenomenon of a flying rabbit. And why? It's simply not in their consciousness yet to know that the destiny of each Soul is to become a Coworker with God, who expects more of us than an eternity of eating and play.

For many, life is much like a trip to a casino. They place all their talents and dreams on the gaming table, then bet the outcome of this life upon a turn of the wheel of fortune. That is the sum of their spiritual life in pursuit of God.

Happiness, to them, is blind luck.

People want happiness, but they go about it backward. They keep looking for happiness. And then they spend their money on things: new computer toys, new cars, new clothes, and the like. Trying to find happiness. If they'd only look for freedom first—maybe meditate like the Buddhists or contemplate as we do in Eckankar. Contemplation is a lighter form of going within than meditation.

Yet some individuals do have a true desire for God and use some form of prayer or worship to better understand the Creator. Mostly, however, their prayer is like traffic on a one-way street: They do all the talking.

It never occurs to them to stop for a moment and listen. God may want to speak.

Often, God doesn't get a word in at all.

How, then, does God communicate with us? God speaks to all life with the voice of divine Light and Sound. The Christian name for these dual aspects of God is the Holy Spirit, or the Holy Ghost, which in Eckankar we refer to by the age-old name ECK.

The range of vibration in the universe spans from infinity to infinity. And while the primal cause of vibration is the Light and Sound of God, the human voice is a mere speck on the full scale of vibration. Why would God only speak in a whisper? Yet people who believe that God speaks chiefly in the frequency range of the human voice forget that the human voice, in comparison to the universe of sound, is but a tiny whisper.

So the idea that God only speaks to life within the narrow field of human sound is an attempt to reduce the might of God.

The Light and Sound of God are the food and drink of saints. Saul of Tarsus, on the road to Damascus, was struck to the earth by the Light of God. Martin Luther, the great reformer, was also fortunate to see It. Then there was Genghis Khan, the Mongol conqueror of the thirteenth century, who every so often would fall into a swoon for days, able only to chant *HU*, an ancient name for God. In those trance states, he saw and heard the majestic Light and Sound of God. The Divine One spoke through the Holy Spirit.

So the highest form of speech from God to the more spiritually advanced of the human race is the Light and Sound.

Who, then, does God talk to?

In fact, everyone who has made a contribution to the human race has heard or seen the True Voice. The ways of God are many. God often speaks in a less direct manner to dreamers, poets, visionaries, and prophets. In part, God's Voice speaks to people through visions or dreams, daydreams, prayer (the listening kind), or intuition.

History tells of many such people.

Brother Lawrence was a Carmelite monk in Paris around 1666. He was the monk whose duty it was to wash the pots and pans. Brother Lawrence found a way to practice the presence of God while washing the pots and pans, doing even the very lowly jobs. The people around him couldn't understand how he could be so happy while doing the dirty work. It was because he saw God in everything he did.

A list of other famous people who have been a mouthpiece for the Voice of God includes the likes of Socrates, Plato, Elijah, King David, Mozart, Beethoven, Jung, Einstein, Shelley, Edison, Michelangelo, and thousands more. Each does his best to render the divine will into human terms, using a natural genius as the tool of communication.

The Sound and Light carry out God's scheme of creation. So the highest anyone can aspire to is a life of high creativity, but always guided by the force of divine love.

That is how to be most like God.

What Is True Prayer?

*C*orrect prayer is listening to God. If a person is going to err in prayer, it's through too much telling or talking to God. There's nothing wrong with telling or asking; there's nothing wrong with talking to God. But after you've asked your question, listen. Be quiet and listen.

Listening is true prayer, prayer of the highest sort. Even prayer where you're asking God something is of a high sort, or it can be. But sometimes people carry it to extremes.

When I was a child, my parents had us say our childhood prayers at bedtime. As I grew up and went to divinity school, I would still say my prayers at night. Not that

11

those of us at divinity school were very righteous. A very small percentage were truly pious, and the rest of us were about average. We got along. We knew God was there. We did our lessons; we did our Bible study and science and math. There were also those in divinity school who were quite nonpious.

I used to say my prayers nightly, but away from home I could try out my wings a little bit. Some nights I'd just lie there and ask God for all kinds of things. I'd ask God for riches. I'd ask God to get rid of my toothaches. They came from all the sugar I ate; I hadn't made the connection between sugar and tooth decay. Every Sunday I'd go to the bakery and buy all this wonderful chocolate, all these jelly-filled rolls—I'd just stuff myself. I'd buy enough for my friends too. It took me years to figure out what I was doing, and I think the toothaches helped. Life has a way of teaching us better.

This is what I learned about prayer: that sometimes there is a wrong sort of prayer. You ask God to take away a toothache, when basically you should stop eating the things that give you the toothache. But that's how we learn.

People ask God to make them rich, and at the same time they squander their money. They have done this their whole lives. What kind of a prayer is that? It's a prayer of irresponsibility. You're not taking responsibility for your own welfare.

Mostly, true prayer is listening to God.

How Does Prayer Work?

*T*he Spindrift Organization has done a lot of experiments in the lab trying to prove that prayer works. They set up experiments with plants, and they tried directed prayer. They'd always have a control group. Then they would see if there were any differences in plant growth. And there were.

They did these experiments for a while, and then somebody had an idea. They said, "We've proved now that prayer changes things." In other words, saying to the little plant, "Grow!" "But now let's see if there's a difference between directed prayer and other types." They wanted to look at another kind of prayer, which is nondirected prayer.

Nondirected prayer is more along the lines of "Thy will be done."

So they took a plate with mold on it. They put it through a quick rinse of alcohol to give the mold a shock, to almost kill it. And then they drew a line right down the center.

Side A was the control side. They wouldn't pray for that side. They asked people to pray for the mold on side B, but not on the order of, "Grow, you little green molds, grow!" They didn't do it like that. They just said, "Thy will be done," regarding the B side.

By doing this truly, people are giving goodwill to life. They're passing along the love of God to other people and things.

They found that nondirected prayer worked even better than directed prayer. Then they did other experiments and got the same results: the nondirected prayer was better than telling God what to do.

15

They also found that some kind of attention was better than nothing at all.

It gets very difficult if you have an illness and say, "God, I need more red blood cells. Produce more red blood cells." It may be exactly the wrong thing. You might need more white blood cells.

Directed prayer doesn't work as well because it depends upon the human consciousness and all its ignorance. But nondirected prayer depends upon the divine power, the higher power. It depends upon the power of God. So whether you say, "Thy will, not mine, be done," or "May the blessings be," this is the proper spiritual way to direct your own life.

You can use it in your own spiritual exercises with a word that you sing to yourself during contemplation (*HU* is a good one—see page 25). You can sing the word, but before you start, you can say, "May the blessings be" or "Thy will be done."

If you have a health problem, or if you're having a problem finding work or keeping the job you have, or if you're having a problem with your loved one or someone not so loved—instead of saying, "God, help me be stronger," maybe just try "Thy will be done."

It's unconditional love that makes such a prayer. And this is important.

What many people don't realize is that God's love, too, is unconditional love. Soul exists because God loves It. That means you exist because God loves you.

THE POWER OF CHANTING

$\mathcal{S}$ome time ago there was a Benedictine monastery in France. The Benedictines are known for their very rigorous schedule of prayer, work, and chanting. They chant from six to eight hours a day, work very hard, and only sleep a little.

This particular monastery got a new abbot. While trying to bring in the reforms of the Second Vatican Council, he made a study of the chanting the monks did.

Eventually the abbot told the monks, "We're chanting from six to eight hours a day. This time could be better spent for something else." And he asked them to stop chanting.

In just a few weeks, the abbot noticed

that the monks looked very fatigued. Everyone was so tired that they could barely continue with their daily schedule. Some thought maybe the fatigue was from working such long hours and getting so little sleep. So the abbot gave them eight instead of four hours of sleep and reduced their workload.

When the fatigue persisted, a medical specialist and a dietitian were called in. They prescribed more meat and potatoes instead of the monks' centuries-old diet of fish and vegetables. Now they not only felt more fatigue, but many of the monks became ill.

Seeing that none of this was working, the abbot finally called in a man who studied sound.

Since this man knew that certain sounds were very beneficial, he told the monks, "Go back to chanting six to eight hours a day. Chanting is what heals you and gives you the strength to keep up your schedule."

The monks began chanting again. They resumed their simple diet and only got four hours of sleep. Within six months, most of them were back on their rigorous schedule, fit as ever.

Most of us don't have the time or inclination to live in a monastery and chant six to eight hours a day. The chant of *HU* is a higher chant, and it gets the same job done in just twenty minutes.

Chanting *HU* gives Soul vitality and strength.

A Healing Light

*L*inda grew up Episcopalian, in the religion of her family. In grade school, she got into Christian Science; in her teen years she came into contact with the Unity teachings.

Then she found out about meditation. Since then she has found Eckankar and become an ECKist. But in the years before ECK, when she was a teenager practicing meditation, someone told her how to work with pictures, to see things as pictures in the Spiritual Eye.

So one day she sat down to do this, and right away she had an experience. She saw a beautiful and pure yellow light, like the most beautiful lemon pie you can imagine.

This was the Light of God, one of the two aspects of the Holy Spirit. The other is the Sound.

When Linda saw this yellow light, it was so beautiful that it healed and uplifted her. She became a part of the light and went into the light. Then after some time—she couldn't remember exactly what had happened—she came back into her body.

"This meditation's OK," she said.

The next day she tried the very same technique again, but she saw nothing except absolute blackness. Worse, she started pushing. She stared into her Spiritual Eye, which is that point right above and between the eyebrows.

And she began to see faces coming out of the blackness, staring back at her. Linda didn't know what these faces were.

Sometimes they were faces she had worn in previous lives. It was as if she were looking at a reflection of herself in a shiny

22

mirror or a pool. Other times they were faces of people who were close to her, with whom she had a karmic tie and a karmic burden. People who would play a part in her life in the future as they had already played a part in the past. The faces frightened her. So after a few more tries to contact the light again, she gave up.

But this was the beginning of her experience with the Light and Sound of God. In the following years, Linda discovered Eckankar, and by using the Spiritual Exercises of ECK, she began to understand her experiences and resolve the karma represented in the faces she had seen. She grew spiritually by taking the path of divine love.

THE MOST BEAUTIFUL PRAYER

A husband and wife in their seventies, whom I'll call Charlie and Hanna, were on vacation in California. Charlie has a heart condition, so they carried oxygen. He had to be very careful not to get into strenuous situations.

As they were driving along the highway on a hot, windy California day, a back tire blew out. Charlie guided the car over to the side of the road and got out. Both of them were wondering, *How are we going to fix the tire?* After a few minutes Hanna said, "We'd better start fixing that tire, because nobody's stopping to help us." Charlie said, "Well, at the service station the lug nuts are put on with pneumatic wrenches. We're not going to get them off ourselves."

Hanna didn't know what to do. She needed to clear her mind; she needed to sing *HU*. HU, this ancient love song to God, is the most beautiful prayer. As you sing *HU*, you're not asking God to help you. You're saying that whatever needs to be in life, you are willing to accept it, no matter what it is. In other words, you're simply saying, "Thy will be done." This is true prayer. Not my will, but Thy will be done. And singing *HU* is one of the ways to do a true prayer.

Hanna went up the road to walk their springer spaniel, and she sang *HU* as she walked. This put her into the higher state, the Soul state. She felt calm and peaceful, full of trust. She came back and told Charlie, "We're going to have to unload our luggage from the trunk, get at the jack, and start changing the tire ourselves."

No sooner had she said this than a battered old pickup truck pulled up right in front of them.

The man who got out was a summertime Santa Claus. He was a big, hefty man and very good-natured. He came up to the couple and said, "What can I do to help you?"

They said, "Well, we need to change the tire."

He said, "I'm here to serve the Lord."

You see how the Holy Spirit works. Hanna had sung *HU*, which was saying, "Not my will, but Thine be done." Then, not understanding what to do next, she went back to the car to do something. You always try to do something. She told Charlie that they would have to do the best they could. But before they could even start, the Holy Spirit sent someone to help them. And one of the first things this person says is, "I'm here to serve the Lord."

The man helped Charlie and Hanna

unload the trunk. Once they got to the jack, the man put it underneath the car, jacked it up, and changed the tire. He fixed everything and helped them put their luggage back in the trunk.

"Thank you very much," said Hanna. "Can I pay you something?"

And the man said, "No charge. I'm just doing the Lord's work."

Beyond Prayer and
Meditation: Contemplation

*B*eyond prayer is contemplation.

Contemplation is a method that enables you to begin to go out and actively explore the inner worlds of your own being. It is different than meditation, a passive state in which the practitioner goes within and just quietly waits for the light.

One contemplative technique is to read something inspirational—a biblical verse or a passage from the ECK writings—then shut your eyes and look inwardly, very gently, at the form of an ECK Master, Jesus, or any figure you feel is a spiritual traveler. Ask to be shown the truth. You can ask for love, wisdom, and understanding, but something greater than these three things, which are only attributes of God, is to ask for the realization of God.

Through contemplation one comes to an understanding of the mental and emotional bodies. There are also other ways to approach life. Another step is to make a study of who and what you are and make an effort to learn the spiritual laws, such as the Law of Cause and Effect.

A third step whereby one can learn about spiritual truths is through service. Service means giving in some way. If you expect to grow spiritually, you have to give of yourself. There is no other way you can unfold spiritually and rise into the high heavens of God.

If you have never used contemplation or a spiritual exercise before, and you would like to compare it to prayer, then pray in the evening before you go to bed, and try a spiritual exercise later. You can look to Jesus or anyone else while following the instructions given for "A Simple Spiritual Exercise to Try" on page 49 or any of the other spiritual exercises included in this book. Try it for yourself, and see if there is a difference between how prayer works for you and how a spiritual exercise works for you.

Spiritual exercises are the way to become more aware of this life. Spiritual exercises, contemplation, and prayer of the right kind are all the same. Basically, it's opening your heart to God or the Holy Spirit and listening.

What we want to do is contact the Voice of God, which is the Holy Spirit. This Voice of God can be known through the Light and Sound that uplifts us so we can reach into the high states of spiritual consciousness. No longer bound by the hand of destiny, we then become spiritually free to mark our own course for this lifetime and into the worlds beyond.

THE TRANSFORMING POWER OF THE SPIRITUAL EXERCISES OF ECK

*T*he Spiritual Exercises of ECK give you confidence in yourself. You learn that you are Soul, you are eternal. Then you know with certainty that you live forever, that death cannot destroy you.

The spiritual exercises work similarly to physical exercises. If you want your body to be strong and healthy, you've got to swim or run or do something to keep fit. For the Soul body, you do the Spiritual Exercises of ECK, a form of inner communication also called contemplation.

These spiritual exercises link you with the guidance of the Holy Spirit, which is seen as Light and heard as Sound. The inner Sound is the Voice of God calling us home. The inner Light is a beacon to light our way. All the Spiritual Exercises of ECK are built on these two divine aspects of the Holy Spirit.

Experiment with them, and try new things. You're in your own God Worlds. I've gone to different extremes with the spiritual exercises, trying very complicated ones I developed for myself, dropping them when they didn't work anymore.

It's like a vein of gold running through a mountain. You're on it for a while, then the vein runs out, and you have to scout around and find another one. Use your creative abilities to go a step further.

Are you learning something new every day from what you're doing? Are you getting insight and help from within? This is what you ought to be working for.

A Guide to the Most Secret Part of Yourself

*T*he most secret part of yourself is the heart of love. The greatest gift life can give you is a means to come into contact with this mysterious part, which is the secret to life itself.

Seekers in ages past discovered and followed a teacher who could guide them beyond the spiritual limitations of body and mind. Countless others, including many saints, have mastered the art and science of Soul Travel.

In Eckankar, an earnest seeker is under the protection of a spiritual guide known as the MAHANTA. This is the Spiritual Traveler.

As the MAHANTA he is the Inner Master, the one who comes on the other planes to impart knowledge, truth, and wisdom.

The MAHANTA is a state of consciousness. It is a spiritual state of consciousness very much like the Buddha consciousness or the Christ consciousness. The Living ECK Master is the other half of the title *the MAHANTA, the Living ECK Master.* This means the outer spiritual teacher, myself.

The teachings of Eckankar speak very directly and very distinctly of the two parts of the Master: the Inner Master and the Outer Master. The Inner Master is the MAHANTA, and the Outer Master is the Living ECK Master.

The Inner Master is not a physical being. It is someone you see in the inner planes during contemplation or in the dream state. He may look like me, he may look like another ECK Master, or he may even look the same as Christ. All it is, really, is the merging of the Light and Sound of God into a matrix, into a form which appears as a person. This, then, becomes the inner guide which steers a person out of the pitfalls of karma, the troubles we make for ourselves through ignorance of the spiritual laws.

The Master often works in the dream state because it is easier to get through. Fears can inhibit and prevent one from exercising the freedom and power and wisdom which are the birthright of Soul. In the dream state, the Inner Master can begin working with you to familiarize and make you comfortable with what comes on the other side.

You can get to the most secret part of yourself through contemplation, through the Spiritual Exercises of ECK. Contemplation is a conversation with the most secret, most genuine, and most mysterious part of yourself.

Help is so close, help is so near. All you have to do is do your part—the spiritual exercises. They are the key. Take the key, and put it in the door of your heart, and the Mahanta will turn the key and open the door.

And the door opens, of course, to God's love—infinite, boundless, refreshing love, like a fountain in the desert.

Kristy, a longtime member of Eckankar, started a business, and she was on a business trip with a friend, a new ECKist. One evening, after a difficult day, they came back to the hotel room. They were recounting all the blessings that the Mahanta had given them during the day. They were talking about one blessing after another. Then they said good night to each other and turned out the light.

Kristy, for her spiritual exercise, began thinking of some of the different names for the Mahanta, and the one that came to mind was the Ancient One.

"The One who comes to wake us up," she said. This is the purpose of the MAHANTA, the Living ECK Master: to awaken Soul. The MAHANTA comes to let Soul know that Its true destiny is to come home again to God. This is Its purpose.

As Kristy was thinking about the MAHANTA, the Ancient One, her friend, the new ECKist, was having her own contemplation. She was using an imagination technique, thinking of a boyfriend and the possibility of their relationship developing. Both Kristy and the new ECKist, her friend, were thinking of love. Their hearts were filled with love as they were doing this contemplation.

Suddenly, in the dark of the room, for no reason whatsoever, the TV went on all by itself. They both sat straight up in bed and looked at it.

On the screen were the words "Thanks for tuning in."

37

They thought maybe somehow the remote control for the TV had gotten into the bed and one of them had rolled over it, and this had turned on the TV. But the remote control was on the desk, far away from the bed.

The new ECKist began laughing. She wasn't afraid of this strange phenomenon. For her, it was assurance of the MAHANTA's divine love for her, speaking to her through the spiritual channels, using whatever was available—the TV set.

The message on the screen, "Thanks for tuning in," meant Thanks for doing your spiritual exercises, because that is Soul's link with God.

QUESTIONS AND ANSWERS

*A*s spiritual leader of Eckankar, I get thousands of letters from seekers of truth around the world. All want direct and useful answers about how to travel the road to God. I reply personally to many of these letters.

Here are several questions I've been asked about prayer, meditation, and contemplation.

Read on for clues that might help you.

Psychic Interference

Is there anything wrong with praying for someone to get well?

If someone asks for help, then it is our choice whether or not to give them whatever information we have. But so often the people who do healings, especially those who know nothing about the laws of Spirit, take it upon themselves to pray for a sick person to get well. That is actually a violation of the spiritual law, but many people feel they are doing it for God and therefore it's right.

Do it if you will, but because you are interfering with another person's spiritual beingness, you are going to pay the price. This is one of the areas in which the orthodox churches have failed the people. They constantly encourage praying for someone else to change their state of consciousness—to find Jesus, to be healed, or whatever.

If these prayers are directed toward a person of greater spiritual evolution, one who is protected by a higher force, there will be consequences. These prayers are really only psychic forces that are shot toward the white light that surrounds the protected one. When these prayers hit the protective light, they bounce straight back to the sender. You will find that the people who do a lot of praying for others usually have plenty of problems themselves. Money doesn't come in right, health isn't good, and family problems arise.

One family back home made it a cause to pray for me to come back to the church. I didn't want to go back to the church. They might as well have been praying for a fourth grader to go back and be a first-grade pupil again. People do this in the mistaken belief that it makes them more spiritual.

Better is nondirected prayer, which means that we're willing to let the Holy Spirit take care of the affairs in life according to the divine plan instead of our personal plan.

The Difference between Meditation and Contemplation

What is the difference between meditation and contemplation?

In meditation, as taught by some of the other paths, you go inwardly and try to become passive and still. This is a first step. But then we begin the creative techniques to try to reach a meeting with the Inner Master in some way.

Using the visualization technique, for instance, we may form a setting for ourselves. We'll see the blades of grass, the clouds, and the trees. We then visualize one of the ECK Masters coming along. We may do it night after night without success, but we keep at it; and eventually it may work so well that we can even feel the wind and smell the flowers.

When Visualization Is Hard

I have trouble visualizing in my contemplation. What can I do?

No one can look closely with the inner vision. It is more a relaxed and easy sensing of the object. The inner vision does not work in the same way as our outer eyes. It goes more keenly into the object, seeing more but with less strain.

Whenever difficulties with visualization come to mind, say firmly to yourself, "I can visualize a little already, so I have only to develop what I already know."

Everyone visualizes unknowingly when looking forward to something. Until you can visualize to your satisfaction, think and feel consciously.

An Appointment with Divine Spirit

When is the best time to pray, meditate, or contemplate?

Christians often say prayers at a certain time. Most of this is done by habit: prayers before meals or, in some families, prayer after meals. Prayers at bedtime. But always at a given time.

I would say this is very important for a person of any faith, because when there is an appointed time, it's like an appointment between you and the source of truth, between you and the Holy Spirit.

Say you have an appointment with someone, a lunch date. You're looking forward to it. The lunch date is at noon. You get there at noon, but the person you're to meet doesn't get there until 1:00 p.m. What kind of a lunch date is that? Something's very off. Or the other person gets there at noon, and you get there at 1:00 p.m. It's not going to be the happiest lunch hour.

It's the same sort of thing with your spiritual exercises. When both parties are at a spiritual meeting at the same time—like the MAHANTA and you, or the Christ Consciousness and you, or Divine Spirit and you—it's like having an appetite for food. If you're used to eating at noon, you're hungry by noon, and you're going to appreciate the food more than if you ate lunch at 10:00 a.m., right after breakfast. Or if you ate lunch later. If you eat lunch one day at 10:00 a.m., the next day at 1:00 p.m., and the next day at 4:00 p.m., pretty soon your body is thrown completely out of balance.

If you want things to be in balance, if you want to be more in tune with the communication from the Holy Spirit, set a time. Make an appointment. This is the time to do your prayer; this is the time to do your meditations; this is the time to do your contemplations.

The Key to Success

How soon can I expect success with the spiritual exercises?

Be patient with yourself. It is a rare person who has instant success and dramatic results right away. Expect subtle, gradual changes in your outlook on life over a period of weeks or months. A good way to keep track of this is by using your journal to note any insights, perceptions, or changes you notice in yourself.

Use the spiritual exercise that works best for you based on the outer conditions you're faced with. No matter which one you use, all you really want is experience with the Light and Sound of God.

Do one exercise every day. Spend about twenty minutes on it. This builds your spiritual stamina gently over time. Regular daily practice is the key to success.

Facing the Bear:
How to Quiet the Mind

It's very hard for me to sit still. Are there spiritual exercises I can do that are more active than silent contemplation?

There's a French proverb that says a good meal ought to begin with hunger. Silent contemplation is the best way. And everyone who hungers for God enough will face the bear and go through the discipline of quieting the mind and stilling the body.

46

Now, I do have to say that there are a lot of hyperactive youth today, and also adults. And much of this is from the electromagnetic things around them—like cell phones, TVs, and so on. They are part of our society, so I'm not saying anything against it. But these definitely do affect the individual's energy, where people become more frantic, more frenetic. So, doing the spiritual exercises for them becomes more difficult, because they've got to still both mind and body.

When the body is going into contemplation, moving from the physical state into the deeper state, it goes through several zones of sensation. These are mainly to do with the physical body. All of a sudden you itch, and you try not to scratch. But the itch comes again, so you might as well scratch it. And then keep your attention on the Inner Master, on the MAHANTA. Put your attention there, and pretty soon you'll

47

get through that zone.

Then you come to another zone that deals with the mind. These are the mental worlds. Now the mind will try to hop around on you. It will jump around the way your body did just a little bit ago. Paul Twitchell, Eckankar's modern-day founder, said it jumps around like a monkey. And it really wants to. Sometimes you can fight it, and sometimes you just watch the monkey jump around.

Try to do the spiritual exercise quietly. Accept the body's need to scratch, and just do it. When you get to the mental or mind part, put your attention on the Master. Then if the mind jumps around too much, just go with it. Watch it. Pretty soon, the mind gets bored. And then maybe you can break through that way.

Spiritual Exercises to Help You on Your Way

A Simple Spiritual Exercise to Try

*T*ry this simple spiritual exercise to help you hear and see the two aspects of God, the Light and Sound.

Go somewhere quiet. Sit or lie down in a comfortable place. Put your attention on your Spiritual Eye, a point just above and behind your eyebrows. With eyes lightly shut, begin to sing a holy word or phrase, such as *HU, God, Holy Spirit,* or *Show me thy ways, O Lord.* But fill your heart with love before you approach the altar of God, because only the pure may come.

Be patient. Do this exercise daily for several weeks, for a limit of twenty minutes each time. Sit, sing, and wait. God speaks only when you are able to listen.

There is more to the pursuit of God than luck.

Monkeys of the Mind

When your mind jumps around, you can visualize your thoughts as monkeys jumping around. See what you can do to make them calm down instead of being mischievous. You're working with an imaginative technique here, which gives you a multitude of possibilities.

Visualize a door that you want to walk through, but you can't because the monkeys are jumping all around in front of it. Say to yourself, I've got to get the monkeys quieted down, and then I can go through the door and enter into the worlds of Light and Sound.

Give the monkeys bright, attractive little toys with bells, or feed them bananas. You can get so involved in quieting the monkeys of the mind that you'll find you're enjoying yourself. Soul is now expressing Itself.

As soon as you get them settled down, make a dash for the door. On the other side is the pure golden Light of God.

The monkeys of the mind are merely the guardians of the door. They'll do everything possible to keep you from going through. Once you figure out a way to calm them down, then you're ready to go beyond into the inner worlds.

Open-Eyed Exercise: Contemplation Is Appreciation

Another word for contemplation is *appreciation*. Think about all the reasons you have to be grateful.

Think about the gifts in your life that have come from God, from the Holy Spirit,

51

that make this life worth living. Think about the adventures that are coming, and be grateful for the strength to meet tomorrow.

Appreciate the gift of life.

True contemplation is reflecting on the blessings of God in your life. It's not complex, there are many ways to do it, and it certainly will enrich you.

Spiritual Goal Setting: The Fifteen Times Exercise

Some of you are fans of the comic-strip character Dilbert. His creator is Scott Adams. Dilbert is a low-level employee in a corporate business, lost in a cubicle somewhere. But he sits back and observes all the silly things that happen in a corporate office, and in this he is very good.

Scott Adams spent seventeen years working in a corporate environment, hidden away in a cubicle, doing the best he could to advance. He realized something after all that time: in order to advance in the company he was in, he not only had to be brilliant, come up with good ideas and good plans, but he also had to be tall and have a good head of hair.

But he was five foot eight, and his hair was thinning. He saw he was in a dead-end job and decided he would like to do something more creative.

He had taken an art class in school, made doodles all the time, and was always thinking, *I would like to be a cartoonist.* He tells this story in the July 1997 issue of *Reader's Digest.*

He gives a technique there which you can easily adapt to a spiritual exercise. For him, this technique is an affirmation. But if you work with it along the spiritual lines, it becomes something more than merely a mental affirmation.

An affirmation is a discipline of the mind only. Whereas contemplation, which is a lighter way of going about opening doors for yourself spiritually, opens the way for the Holy Spirit to help you change your life according to Its will. So whenever you do a spiritual exercise of this sort, do it with the attitude "Thy will be done." That lifts it from a simple mental affirmation into true contemplation.

Scott Adams says he thought it important to affirm his goal in writing. So every day he'd write that goal fifteen times: "I will become a syndicated cartoonist."

But he didn't just sit back and wait for the world to find him. He sent some cartoon strips of Dilbert out to a number of syndicates. He got back a lot of rejection slips, but a very big syndicate accepted his idea. And that was the beginning of *Dilbert.*

His technique was based upon the principle of focusing on a goal. He focused by writing that goal down very clearly, fifteen times every day.

How do you do this with a spiritual goal? Simply put your spiritual goals into words, and fashion a spiritual writing exercise on them. For example: "I am a healthy, happy, spiritual being." Or, "I travel in my dreams." Or you can say, "I know the secret of divine love."

Write down your goal fifteen times every day. Then observe things happening that will make that objective more likely to materialize.

Advanced Spiritual Exercise to Lead You into Deeper Levels

In using the following technique, you will find the path to the other worlds illuminated by Soul's own light, much as the headlights of a car, cutting through the darkness of night, illuminate the road ahead. This technique utilizes the seeing power of Soul.

Sit in silence, with the attention fixed on the Spiritual Eye. Put your attention on the Light of God, the white light within the door of the Spiritual Eye. This is the subtle gateway to the Astral world, the first door you will pass through on the way to higher worlds.

With your attention fixed on this door, look obliquely—not directly—at whatever appears on the screen of the mind. If you look at it directly, it will disappear. But if you look at it from an angle, the image of the light will stay.

Now, very softly begin to sing the word for each plane that you must pass through in order to reach the Soul region.

These are: *Alayi* (Physical Plane), *Kala* (Astral Plane), *Mana* (Causal Plane), *Aum* (Mental Plane), *Baju* (Etheric Plane), and *SUGMAD* (Soul Plane). By these sounds you are able to lift yourself up through the corresponding planes into the Soul world.

The God Worlds of ECK

	(Plane)	(Chant)	(Sound)
	ANAMI LOK	HU (*HYOO*)	HU
	AGAM LOK	HUK (*HOOK*)	MUSIC OF WOODWINDS
	HUKIKAT LOK	ALUK (*ah-LOOK*)	THOUSAND VIOLINS
	ALAYA LOK	HUM (*HYOOM*)	HUMMING SOUND
	ALAKH LOK	SHANTI (*SHAHN-tee*)	WIND
	ATMA LOK (Soul Plane)	SUGMAD (*SOOG-mahd*)	SINGLE NOTE OF A FLUTE

HIGHER WORLDS POSITIVE — GOD-REALIZATION

LOWER WORLDS NEGATIVE — SELF-REALIZATION

ETHERIC (Intuition) BAJU (*BAH-joo*) BUZZING BEES
The last barrier between the lower worlds and the pure positive God Worlds.

MENTAL (Mind) AUM (*AHM or ah-UHM*) RUNNING WATER
Source of all mental teachings, aesthetics, philosophies, conventional concepts of God, cosmic consciousness.

CAUSAL (Memory) MANA (*MAH-nah*) TINKLING BELLS
Plane where memories, karmic patterns, and Akashic records are stored. The Causal body is also the seed body. Plane of negative reality, which affects all below.

ASTRAL (Emotion) KALA (*kah-LAH*) ROAR OF THE SEA
Source of all psychic phenomena—ghosts, flying saucers, spirits, ESP. Plane reached by astral projection and most occult sciences.

PHYSICAL (Senses) ALAYI (*ah-LAH-yee*) THUNDER
Plane where Soul is trapped by the five passions: lust, anger, greed, vanity, and attachment. Plane of time, space, and matter. Illusion of reality.

The Light of God appears on all planes, but the light that should interest you most is the Blue Star. It will come into focus after the technique has been practiced for a certain length of time. This star represents the MAHANTA, the Living ECK Master, who will later appear in his radiant body.

Sometimes the Master appears as a blue star, sometimes as a misty, pale blue light. The star or light will lead you gently through the various planes into the Soul region. You must trust It completely, never being doubtful or hesitant about following It, nor wondering where It may lead you.

As Soul gets collected and concentrates on the Spiritual Eye, you will have some preliminary experiences of the inner sounds and sights. These occur before Soul is settled down and actually traveling in the inner worlds. You may hear sounds similar to a moving train, whistles, or stringed instruments. Then you will hear sounds like the tinkling of small bells, progressing to the ringing notes of a large bell. Following this are lights similar to the glowing of charcoal, then lightning, and finally the gigantic star.

Then you are able to see a whole starry sky. You see the Lightning and Moon Worlds, and you are ready for the ascent. You may see such forms as mist, smoke, suns, fire, winds, fireflies, lightning, crystals, and moons. Your attention may be scattered at this point, but bring it back and focus again on a single point.

The Light and Sound are the vision and the music of God. Each time they come to you, you are lifted in spiritual consciousness.

This is what you do in contemplation, in your fifteen to twenty minutes a day. You listen for the Voice of God and watch for some appearance of the Light of God.

When the Light and Sound come into the inner vision, the Spiritual Eye, or the heart, you'll be filled with a joy and love you've never felt before.

Next Steps in Spiritual Exploration

- **Try a spiritual exercise.**
  Review the spiritual exercises in this book.
  Experiment with them.

- **Browse our website: www.Eckankar.org.**
  Watch videos; get free books, answers to
  FAQs, and more info.

- **Attend an Eckankar event** in your area.
  Visit "Find a Location" (under "Engage") on
  our website.

- **Enroll** in an ECK Advanced Spiritual Living
  course.

- **Read additional books** about the ECK
  teachings.

- **Call us:** Call 1-800-LOVE GOD (1-800-568-
  3463, toll-free, automated) or (952) 380-2222
  (direct).

- **Write to:** ECKANKAR, Dept. BK71, PO Box
  2000, Chanhassen, MN 55317-2000 USA.

For Further Reading
By Harold Klemp

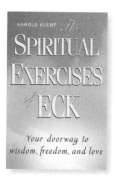

The Spiritual Exercises of ECK

This book is a staircase with 131 steps leading to the doorway to spiritual freedom, self-mastery, wisdom, and love. A comprehensive volume of spiritual exercises for every need.

ECK Wisdom on Conquering Fear

Would having more courage and confidence help you make the most of this lifetime?

Going far beyond typical self-help advice, this book invites you to explore divine love as the antidote to anxiety and the doorway to inner freedom.

You will discover ways to identify the karmic roots

of fear and align with your highest ideals.

Use this book to soar beyond your limitations and reap the benefits of self-mastery.

Live life to its fullest potential!

ECK Wisdom on Dreams

This dream study will help you be more *awake* than you've ever been!

ECK Wisdom on Dreams reveals the most ancient of dream teachings for a richer and more productive life today.

In this dynamic book, author Harold Klemp shows you how to remember your dreams, apply dream wisdom to everyday situations, recognize prophetic dreams, and more.

You will be introduced to the art of dream interpretation and offered techniques to discover the treasures of your inner worlds.

ECK Wisdom on Health and Healing

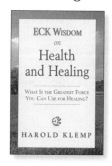

This book is rich with spiritual keys to better health on every level.

Discover the spiritual roots of illness and how gratitude can open your heart to God's love and healing.

Simple spiritual exercises go deep to help you get personal divine guidance and insights.

Revitalize your connection with the true healing power of God's love.

ECK Wisdom on Inner Guidance

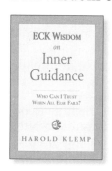

Looking for answers, guidance, protection?

Help can come as a nudge, a dream, a vision, or a quiet voice within you. This book offers new ways to connect with the ever-present guidance of ECK, the Holy Spirit. Start today!

Discover how to listen to the Voice of God; attune to your True Self; work with an inner guide; benefit

63

from dreams, waking dreams, and Golden-tongued Wisdom; and ignite your creativity to solve problems.

Each story, technique, and spiritual exercise is a doorway to greater confidence and love for life.

Open your heart, and let God's voice speak to you!

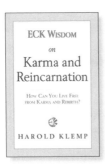

ECK Wisdom on Karma and Reincarnation

Have you lived before? What is the real meaning of life?

Discover your divine destiny—to move beyond the limits of karma and reincarnation and gain spiritual freedom.

This book reveals the purpose of living and the keys to spiritual growth.

You'll find answers to age-old questions about fate, destiny, and free will. These gems of wisdom can enhance your relationships, health, and happiness—and offer the chance to resolve all your karma in this lifetime!

ECK Wisdom on Life after Death

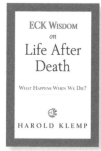

All that lies ahead is already within your heart.

ECK Wisdom on Life after Death invites you to explore the eternal nature of *you*!

Author Harold Klemp offers you new perspectives on seeing heaven before you die, meeting with departed loved ones, near-death experiences, getting help from spiritual guides, animals in heaven, and dealing with grief.

Try the techniques and spiritual exercise included in this book to find answers and explore the secrets of life after death—for yourself.

ECK Wisdom on Relationships

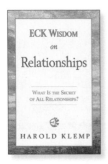

Find the answers to common questions of the heart, including the truth about soul mates, how to strengthen a marriage, and how to know if a partnership is worth developing.

The spiritual exercises included in this book can help you break a pattern of poor relationships and find balance. You'll learn new ways to open your heart to love and enrich your relationship with God.

This book is a key for anyone wanting more love to give, more love to get. It's a key to better relationships with everyone in your life.

ECK Wisdom on Solving Problems

Problems? Problems! Why do we have so many? What causes them? Can we avoid them?

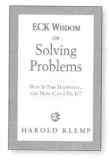

Author Harold Klemp, the spiritual leader of Eckankar, can help you answer these questions and more. His sense of humor and practical approach offer spiritual keys to unlock the secrets to effective problem solving. Learn creative, time-tested techniques to

- find the root cause of a problem;
- change your viewpoint and overcome difficulties;
- conquer your fears;
- work beyond symptoms to solutions;
- kindle your creativity;
- master your karma, past and present;
- receive spiritual guidance that can transform the way you see yourself and your life.

ECK Wisdom on Soul Travel

Where do you go when you close your eyes?

Nowhere? Are you sure?

What about when you daydream?

You go places, don't you?

What about when you close your eyes at night—and dream? When dreams seem more real than everyday life?

That's Soul Travel. It's a natural process that opens the door to the incredible universes where we truly live and have our being. You are Soul, a divine spark of God. The more attention you give to this wonderful truth, the closer you get to the very heart of God.

You learn how to grow in love and awareness. And that's what life is all about, isn't it?

ECK Wisdom on Soul Travel gives you tools to experiment with and introduces you to a spiritual guide who can show you the road to your infinite future—a road that courses through every moment of your daily life.

Take a peek, and explore your own adventure of a lifetime!

ECK Wisdom on Spiritual Freedom

Are you everything you want to be? You came into this life to spread your wings and live in freedom—heart, mind, and Soul!

Author Harold Klemp puts the tools of spiritual freedom firmly in your grasp:

- Keys to embrace the highest expression of who you really are

- Techniques to tap into the divine Life Force for unlimited creativity and problem solving

- New paradigms to reveal the power of loving yourself, God, and all of life

What would you give for the secret of true freedom? Consider this book a ticket to an unexpected destination—the heart of your being.

Open your wings, and prepare for flight!

The Call of Soul

Discover how to find spiritual freedom in this lifetime and the infinite world of God's love for you. Includes a CD with dream and Soul Travel techniques.

Past Lives, Dreams, and Soul Travel

These stories and exercises help you find your true purpose, discover greater love than you've ever known, and learn that spiritual freedom is within reach.

The Mahanta Transcripts Series

The Mahanta Transcripts, books 1–18, are from Harold Klemp's talks at Eckankar seminars. He has taught thousands how to have a natural, direct relationship with the Holy Spirit. The stories and wonderful insights contained in these talks will lead you to deeper spiritual understanding.

Autobiography of a Modern Prophet

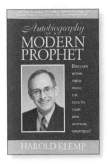

This riveting story of Harold Klemp's climb up the Mountain of God will help you discover the keys to your own spiritual greatness.

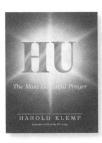

HU, the Most Beautiful Prayer

Singing *HU*, the ancient name for God, can open your heart and lead you to a new understanding of yourself. Includes a CD of the HU song.

Those Wonderful ECK Masters

Would you like to have *personal* experience with spiritual Masters that people all over the world—since the beginning of time—have looked to for guidance, protection, and divine love? This book includes real-life stories and spiritual exercises to meet eleven ECK Masters.

The Sound of Soul

Sacred Sound, ancient mantra. HU is a universal love song to God; it brings alignment with your true purpose and highest good. This potent volume of contemplation seeds and spiritual exercises can get you started on the journey of a lifetime—your return to the heart of God.

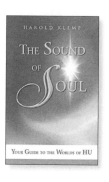

GLOSSARY

Words set in SMALL CAPS are defined elsewhere in this glossary.

Blue Light   How the MAHANTA often appears in the inner worlds to the CHELA or seeker.

chela   A spiritual student, often a member of ECKANKAR.

ECK   The Life Force, Holy Spirit, or Audible Life Current which sustains all life.

Eckankar *EHK-ahn-kahr*   The Path of Spiritual Freedom. Also known as the Ancient Science of SOUL TRAVEL. A truly spiritual way of life for the individual in modern times. The teachings provide a framework for anyone to explore their own spiritual experiences. Established by PAUL TWITCHELL, the modern-day founder, in 1965. The word means Coworker with God.

ECK Masters   Spiritual Masters who can assist and protect people in their spiritual studies and travels. The ECK Masters are from a long line of God-Realized SOULS who know the responsibility that goes with spiritual freedom.

74

God-Realization   The state of God Consciousness. Complete and conscious awareness of God.

HU *HYOO*   The most ancient, secret name for God. It can be sung as a love song to God aloud or silently to oneself to align with God's love.

initiation   Earned by a member of ECKANKAR through spiritual unfoldment and service to God. The initiation is a private ceremony in which the individual is linked to the Sound and Light of God.

Karma, Law of   The Law of Cause and Effect, action and reaction, justice, retribution, and reward, which applies to the lower or psychic worlds: the Physical, Astral, Causal, Mental, and Etheric PLANES.

Klemp, Harold   The present MAHANTA, the LIVING ECK MASTER. SRI Harold Klemp became the MAHANTA, the Living ECK Master in 1981. His spiritual name is WAH Z.

Living ECK Master   The spiritual leader of ECKANKAR. He leads SOUL back to God. He teaches in the physical world as the Outer Master, in the dream state as the Dream Master, and in the spiritual worlds as the Inner Master. SRI HAROLD KLEMP became the MAHANTA, the Living ECK Master in 1981.

75

MAHANTA   An expression of the Spirit of God that is always with you. Sometimes seen as the BLUE LIGHT or Blue Star or in the form of the MAHANTA, the LIVING ECK MASTER. The highest state of God Consciousness on earth, only embodied in the Living ECK Master. He is the Living Word.

planes   Levels of existence, such as the Physical, Astral, Causal, Mental, Etheric, and SOUL Planes.

Rebazar Tarzs   A Tibetan ECK MASTER known as the Torchbearer of ECKANKAR in the lower worlds.

Satsang   A class in which students of ECK study a monthly lesson from ECKANKAR.

Self-Realization   SOUL recognition. The entering of Soul into the Soul PLANE and there beholding Itself as pure Spirit. A state of Seeing, Knowing, and Being.

Shariyat-Ki-Sugmad   Way of the Eternal; the sacred scriptures of ECKANKAR. The scriptures are comprised of twelve volumes in the spiritual worlds. The first two were transcribed from the inner PLANES by PAUL TWITCHELL, modern-day founder of Eckankar.

Soul   The True Self, an individual, eternal spark of God. The inner, most sacred part of each person. Soul can see, know, and perceive all things. It is the creative center of Its own world.

Soul Travel   The expansion of consciousness. The ability of SOUL to transcend the physical body and travel into the spiritual worlds of God. Soul Travel is taught only by the LIVING ECK MASTER. It helps people unfold spiritually and can provide proof of the existence of God and life after death.

Sound and Light of ECK   The Holy Spirit. The two aspects through which God appears in the lower worlds. People can experience them by looking and listening within themselves and through SOUL TRAVEL.

Spiritual Exercises of ECK   Daily practices for direct, personal experience with the God Current. Creative techniques using contemplation and the singing of sacred words to bring the higher awareness of SOUL into daily life.

Sri   A title of spiritual respect, similar to reverend or pastor, used for those who have attained the Kingdom of God. In ECKANKAR, it is reserved for the MAHANTA, the LIVING ECK MASTER.

SUGMAD   *SOOG-mahd*   A sacred name for God. It is the source of all life, neither male nor female, the Ocean of Love and Mercy.

Temples of Golden Wisdom Golden Wisdom Temples found on the various PLANES—from the Physical to the Anami Lok; CHELAS of ECKANKAR are taken to these temples in the SOUL body to be educated in the divine knowledge; sections of the SHARIYAT-KI-SUGMAD, the sacred teachings of ECK, are kept at these temples.

Twitchell, Paul An American ECK MASTER who brought the modern teachings of ECKANKAR to the world through his writings and lectures. His spiritual name is Peddar Zaskq.

Wah Z *WAH zee* The spiritual name of SRI HAROLD KLEMP. It means the secret doctrine. It is his name in the spiritual worlds.

Z *ZEE* Spiritual name for SRI HAROLD KLEMP. *See also* WAH Z.

For more explanations of ECKANKAR terms, see *A Cosmic Sea of Words: The ECKANKAR Lexicon*, by Harold Klemp.

ABOUT THE AUTHOR

Award-winning author, teacher, and spiritual guide Sri Harold Klemp helps seekers reach their full potential.

He is the MAHANTA, the Living ECK Master and spiritual leader of Eckankar, the Path of Spiritual Freedom. He is the latest in a long line of spiritual Adepts who have served throughout history in every culture of the world.

Sri Harold teaches creative spiritual practices that enable anyone to achieve life mastery and gain inner peace and contentment. His messages are relevant to today's spiritual needs and resonate with every generation.

Sri Harold's body of work includes more than one hundred books, which have been translated into eighteen languages and won multiple awards. The miraculous, true-life stories he shares lift the veil between heaven and earth.

In his groundbreaking memoir, *Autobiography of a Modern Prophet,* he reveals secrets to spiritual success gleaned from his personal journey into the heart of God.

Find your own path to true happiness, wisdom, and love in Sri Harold Klemp's inspired writings.